HOUSE OF ABUNDANCE
PUBLICATIONS

Rolling Beyond the Horizon

Fascinating Facts About Trains

First edition

This book was professionally typeset on Reedsy.
Find out more at reedsy.com

"The allure of trains lies in the anticipation of the unknown that lies beyond the next bend."

Edward Thomas

Contents

1

Introduction

Welcome to the World of Trains

From the earliest whispers of the industrial revolution to the high-speed, high-tech marvels that crisscross continents today, trains have been integral to our global narrative. They've brought countries, cultures, and individuals closer together, driving forward commerce, tourism, and exploration. They've bridged lands and hearts, weaving stories of human ingenuity and ambition. "Rolling Beyond the Horizon: Fascinating Facts About Trains" is an exploration of this fantastic journey, a celebration of these iron horses that continue to charm us, and a tribute to the indomitable human spirit that crafted them.

In this book, we will embark on a journey that promises to be as exhilarating and fascinating as a cross-country train ride. We will explore the past, exploring how trains and railways evolved from humble beginnings. We will unlock the mechanics of trains, understanding how they function and move. We will admire the world's most iconic trains and the scenic routes they traverse. Finally, we will look towards the future, envisioning what might lie ahead for trains and railways.

Hold on to your seats as we depart on this exciting journey, discovering why trains are more than just a means of transportation. They are a testament to human curiosity, a monument to our technological prowess, and a symbol of our relentless quest to connect and progress. Welcome aboard, and let's enjoy this ride through the world of trains.

A Brief History of Rail Transportation

Long before the technological marvels we wonder at today, the concept of a 'train' was introduced in the early mines of the United Kingdom. The initial iterations, 'wagonways,' were primitive rail tracks to transport goods. The wheels of progress turned rapidly, leading to a breakthrough invention in the 18th century—the steam engine.

Scottish inventor James Watt revolutionized transportation by adapting the steam engine in 1769. However, George Stephenson incorporated this technology into the railway industry, creating the world's first successful steam-powered locomotive in 1814.

With the steam locomotive's success, the rail travel age began earnestly. The 1800s marked a period of exponential expansion of railway networks, reaching every corner of Britain and soon spilling over to other parts of Europe and North America. The railway mania had begun, with countries racing to create more extensive and efficient railway systems.

By the late 19th and early 20th centuries, steam gave way to electricity and diesel, enabling trains to reach incredible speeds and carry heavier loads. The era of luxurious train travel had arrived, with legendary names like the Orient Express and the Trans-Siberian Railway capturing the public's imagination.

The latter half of the 20th century ushered in an era of high-speed rail travel. The Japanese Shinkansen, also known as the 'Bullet Train,' started this trend in 1964, transforming the perception of train travel with its speed, efficiency, and comfort.

Today, trains are ubiquitous in our lives, serving as a vital mode of transportation for billions of people worldwide. From the humble goods carriage to the supersonic maglev trains, the journey is a testament to human ingenuity and progress, demonstrating our constant quest for faster, safer, and more efficient transportation.

In the following chapters, we will dive deeper into this rich history, exploring the iconic trains, the engineering accomplishments, the scenic rail routes, and the future of train travel. So stay aboard as we continue our journey through the chronicles of rail history.

2

Invention and Evolution of Trains

Early Days of Railways

The conception of rail transport has its roots in the primitive mining railways, colloquially referred to as 'wagonways.' These early railway systems date back to the 16th century in the United Kingdom, where wooden rails served as tracks for horse-drawn wagons laden with ore. Although rudimentary, these wagonways set the stage for a transportation revolution to transform the world.

The turning point, however, came in the 18th century with the invention of the steam engine. The pivotal figure behind this development was James Watt. Although Watt did not directly apply his creation to rail transportation, his steam engine laid the foundation for what would become the cornerstone of the railway industry.

George Stephenson, an English engineer, seized the potential of Watt's invention. Often hailed as the 'Father of Railways,'

Stephenson incorporated the steam engine into rail transport, resulting in the world's first successful steam-powered loco-motive in 1814. His locomotive, known as the 'Blücher,' could haul 30 tons of coal uphill at 4 miles per hour, an unprecedented feat at the time.

The success of the 'Blücher' fueled an exponential expansion of the railway system in the United Kingdom. The 'Stockton and Darlington Railway' and the 'Liverpool and Manchester Railway,' both built by Stephenson, served as prototypes for railway systems worldwide. By the mid-19th century, the railway mania had peaked, with thousands of miles of rail being laid down across the UK and, soon after, in the rest of Europe and North America.

Transition to Diesel and Electric

By the late 19th and early 20th centuries, the Industrial Revo-lution had undergone monumental changes, and rail transport was no exception. Steam engines, while revolutionary in their time, had limitations. They were fuel-hungry, requiring copious amounts of coal and water. Moreover, their maintenance was demanding, and the thick smoke they belched was a growing environmental concern. It was time for another transformation in rail transport technology, leading to the advent of diesel and electric trains.

Diesel engines first emerged in the late 19th century. Still, it was in the 20th century that they found their way into locomotives. Unlike steam engines, diesel locomotives didn't require frequent stops for water. They were also more efficient, converting a higher percentage of the fuel's energy into motion. Also, diesel engines were more reliable and required less maintenance than their steam counterparts.

Around the same time, electric trains began to surface, primarily in urban areas where short-distance travel was prevalent. Electric locomotives were clean, efficient, and quick, ideal for densely populated areas. Early electric trains ran on direct current (DC). Still, the advent of alternating current (AC) technology in the late 19th century dramatically increased their efficiency and range.

The transition to diesel and electric power took time to occur. Steam, diesel, and electric locomotives coexisted for several decades, each serving different needs. However, diesel and electric trains' superior efficiency, reliability, and environmental friendliness gradually led to their widespread adoption. By the mid-20th century, they had primarily supplanted steam locomotives, forever changing the face of rail transport.

As we move on to the next section, we will explore the culmination of these technological advancements—the era of high-speed trains, which brought unprecedented speed and comfort to rail transport, effectively shrinking the world.

Advent of High-Speed Rail

The quest for faster, more efficient modes of transportation is a constant in human history. In the realm of rail transport, this pursuit culminated in the advent of high-speed rail (HSR), forever transforming the landscape of global travel.

The roots of high-speed rail can be traced back to the early 20th century, but the concept took off in post-WWII Japan. With the nation's rapid economic recovery, there was a pressing need for faster, more efficient intercity travel. This led to the development of the Shinkansen, or "Bullet Train," the world's first dedicated high-speed railway system. Unveiled at the 1964 Tokyo Olympics, the Shinkansen was a technological wonder that could reach 210 km/h (130 mph), nearly double the speed of conventional trains.

Inspired by Japan's success, other nations pursued their own high-speed rail projects. In France, the TGV (Train à Grande Vitesse, or "High-Speed Train") was launched in the early 1980s, quickly setting new speed records. Since then, other countries, including Germany, Spain, Italy, China, and Korea, have developed their own high-speed rail networks, each with its unique technologies and innovations.

High-speed rail brought a host of benefits. Providing rapid, reliable, and comfortable intercity travel became a competitive alternative to air travel and long-distance road transport. Moreover, high-speed rail has profoundly impacted economic development, urbanization, and even cultural exchange by connecting cities and regions.

The development of high-speed rail also spurred technological advancements. Each generation of high-speed trains brings new innovations, from aerodynamic train designs to advanced rail infrastructure and state-of-the-art control systems to sophisticated passenger amenities.

3

Mechanics of Trains

Anatomy of a Train

The heart of any train is its locomotive. Powered by various energy sources, including steam, diesel, electricity, or even magnets, locomotives provide the propulsive force that enables a train to move. Locomotives house the engine or motor, the driver's cabin, and other essential operation, control, and safety systems.

Next are the rail cars or carriages, which come in various forms to serve different purposes. Passenger cars are equipped with seating or sleeping arrangements for passengers. In contrast, freight cars are designed to carry a variety of goods ranging from raw materials to finished products. There are also specialized cars, like the dining car, observation car, and baggage car.

You'll often find the caboose at the end of a traditional train. Historically, the caboose served as the office for the train's conductor and the living quarters for the crew. It also provided a vantage point for observing the safe operation of the train.

However, in modern trains, cabooses are primarily obsolete, replaced by electronic detection systems for monitoring train integrity.

Couplers and drawbars connect all these components, allowing for relative movement between the cars to prevent derailment during turns. The wheels, or the wheelsets, are specially designed to bear the train's weight and guide it along the tracks.

The train tracks, also known as the permanent way, are an integral part of the train system. The tracks, consisting of rails, sleepers (or ties), and ballast, provide a stable and smooth surface for the train.

Lastly, trains are equipped with various control, safety, and passenger comfort systems. These include braking, suspension, control, and HVAC (heating, ventilation, and air conditioning) systems.

How Trains Move

How does something as massive as a train actually move? The simple answer is that it relies on three fundamental principles of physics: force, inertia, and friction.

Force is the push or pull that causes an object to move, slow down, speed up, or change direction. In trains, this force is produced by the engine of the locomotive. Depending on the type of train, the engine can be powered by steam, diesel, electricity, or even magnetic fields (as in the case of maglev trains).

The principle of inertia states that an object in motion tends to stay in motion, and an object at rest tends to remain at rest unless acted on by an external force. In the context of trains, this means that once a train is set in motion, it wants to keep moving. And conversely, when a train is stationary, it wants to remain static. This is why a considerable amount of force is required to set a stationary train in motion and, similarly, to bring a moving train to a halt.

Finally, friction plays a crucial role in train movement. Friction is the opposing force that acts when two surfaces come into contact and hinders their relative motion. On the one hand, friction is beneficial as it prevents the wheels of the train from slipping on the tracks, thus allowing the train to move forward. On the other hand, too much friction can cause wear and tear on the train's components, leading to increased maintenance requirements and reduced efficiency.

Also, trains are designed to take advantage of the reduced friction between steel wheels and steel tracks, allowing them to transport heavy loads over long distances with relatively little energy. The conical shape of train wheels also helps the train follow the track and negotiate curves without complex steering mechanisms.

In the next section, we'll discuss the different types of propulsion used in trains and how they leverage these physics principles to move trains effectively and efficiently.

Modern Train Technologies

In the ever-evolving world of train technology, innovations redefine what is possible. Two of the most noteworthy advancements include Magnetic Levitation, more commonly known as Maglev, and Automated Trains.

Magnetic Levitation (Maglev)

Maglev trains represent a significant leap forward in train technology. These trains do not run on traditional tracks; instead, they levitate over guideways using the power of magnetism, eliminating the friction between the train and the track. This drastically reduces energy consumption and allows the train to achieve incredible speeds, with some commercial maglev trains reaching speeds above 375 miles per hour (600 km/h).

The concept of magnetic levitation is relatively simple. The train is lifted by a magnetic field created by electromagnets in the guideway. Once the train is raised, another set of electromagnets is used to push the train forward. The same magnetic field that lifts the train also helps to stabilize and guide it along the guideway.

Automated Trains

Automation technology has brought about a new era in train operation. Automated trains use sophisticated computer systems to control the operation of the train, reducing or even eliminating the need for human operators. These systems handle everything from speed and braking to door operation and announcements.

The benefits of automated trains are numerous. They can run more frequently and with greater precision than trains operated by humans, increasing efficiency and capacity. They can also work around the clock, leading to improved service availability. Moreover, automated systems can react faster than humans in case of a problem, potentially improving safety.

However, adopting automated trains also presents challenges regarding safety and public acceptance. As such, while fully automated trains are becoming increasingly common in controlled environments such as airport shuttles and some metro systems, many passengers still retain human operators, even if they have automated systems.

These are just a few examples of the exciting advancements in train technology. In the following chapter, we will explore how these technologies are being used to shape the future of rail transportation.

4

The World's Most Noteworthy Trains

Iconic Trains and Their Stories

Trains have played a vital role in shaping human history, and some of them have gained an iconic status due to their unique features, historical significance, or intriguing stories associated with them. This section explores some of these iconic trains.

The Orient Express

Few trains in history have captured the imagination, like the Orient Express. This legendary long-distance passenger train service started in 1883, connecting Paris with Istanbul and traversing through some of Europe's most beautiful and culturally rich regions. The train has been a setting for numerous novels, including Agatha Christie's famous detective story "Murder on the Orient Express."

The Flying Scotsman

This iconic British steam locomotive, named after the London to Edinburgh service, is renowned for setting two world records for steam traction: becoming the first steam locomotive to officially reach 100 miles per hour (160 km/h) in 1934 and setting a record for the longest non-stop run by a steam locomotive in 1989.

The Trans-Siberian Railway

This is the longest railway line in the world, spanning a length of 9,289 kilometers (5,772 miles) from Moscow to Vladivostok. This journey offers stunning views of the vast Siberian wilderness. It is often described as the trip of a lifetime, crossing eight time zones and two continents.

Shinkansen

Also known as the "bullet train," Japan's Shinkansen is a network of high-speed railway lines symbolizing efficiency, punctuality, and technological prowess. Since its introduction in 1964, the Shinkansen has transformed travel in Japan and set new benchmarks for high-speed rail travel worldwide.

The Rocky Mountaineer

A luxury tourist train that travels through the heart of the Canadian Rockies, offering some of the most breathtaking scenic views in the world. This journey is not just about reaching the destination; it's about immersing in the rugged beauty of nature, making it a bucket-list item for many train travel enthusiasts.

Bullet Trains - Pioneers of High-Speed Rail

Bullet trains are synonymous with speed, efficiency, and cutting-edge technology. They symbolize the epitome of advancements in railway transportation, beginning in Japan and spreading across Europe. This section goes beyond the basic introduction of bullet trains and dives into their unique features, design elements, and socio-economic impact.

Aerodynamic Design and State-of-the-art Engineering

The bullet trains boast an exceptional aerodynamic design and exemplify state-of-the-art engineering. The streamlined shape of these high-speed marvels significantly reduces air resistance, allowing them to glide effortlessly through the air, achieving remarkable speeds while ensuring optimal energy efficiency. Behind their sleek exteriors lies a testament to meticulous engineering, as lightweight materials and advanced technologies are carefully integrated to enhance stability and safety during rapid transit. These innovative feats of engineering not only redefine the realm of train travel and exemplify a harmonious blend of cutting-edge design and functionality.

Superior Control Systems

Bullet trains employ sophisticated control systems to maintain optimum speed, smooth acceleration and deceleration, and timely arrivals. We'll discuss the automatic train control (ATC) system that prevents over-speeding and ensures a safe distance between trains, contributing to their near-flawless safety record.

Revolutionizing Travel

Bullet trains have transformed how people perceive distance and time, making it feasible to live in one city and commute daily to another hundreds of kilometers away. We will explore the profound impact on urban development, tourism, and regional economies.

Environmental Impact

In an age of growing environmental consciousness, bullet trains offer a more sustainable mode of transportation, consuming significantly less energy per passenger-kilometer than planes or cars. We'll consider the broader environmental implications of high-speed rail networks, from reducing air pollution and traffic congestion to promoting low-carbon urban development.

Challenges and Controversies

Despite the apparent benefits, high-speed rail projects have also faced criticism and challenges, including high construction and maintenance costs, noise pollution, and displacement of local communities.

The remarkable success of bullet trains in Japan and Europe has sparked a wave of similar projects around the globe, heralding a new era in rail transportation. Yet, despite this momentum, the path toward establishing a comprehensive global high-speed rail network is riddled with challenges that demand attention. To fully unlock the potential of this promising technology, these hurdles must be carefully addressed and overcome.

Future of Trains: Hyperloop and Beyond

As we venture into the latter part of our railway journey, we transition from established train technology to cutting-edge innovations poised to redefine our concepts of speed, efficiency, and eco-friendliness in rail travel. The star of this anticipatory panorama is Elon Musk's Hyperloop concept - a proposed transport system that, with its extraordinary features, seems more like a flight of science fiction than an extension of traditional rail systems. Let's embark on this exciting exploration into the future of trains.

What is Hyperloop?

The Hyperloop concept involves a system of pressurized tubes maintaining near-vacuum conditions. Capsules or 'pods' carrying passengers or freight travel within these tubes, with the lack of air resistance allowing for extremely high speeds. The section outlines the concept, its origin, and the physics principles that underpin it.

From Idea to Reality

In 2013, Elon Musk introduced the Hyperloop concept, and numerous companies worldwide are pursuing its realization. This article explores the journey of this revolutionary idea from conception to actuality, providing an overview of the ongoing projects and the diverse stages of their development.

Speed, Efficiency, and Sustainability

The Hyperloop promises to transport passengers at unprecedented speeds - potentially exceeding 700 mph. Furthermore, it is projected to be powered by renewable energy sources, making it a highly sustainable mode of transportation.

Challenges and Critiques

As captivating as the Hyperloop concept may be, it encounters substantial technical and regulatory hurdles. Overcoming challenges such as establishing and sustaining near-vacuum conditions across vast distances and ensuring passenger safety during high-speed travel proves daunting.

Beyond Hyperloop

While Hyperloop represents the most futuristic vision of rail transport, other innovations are also transforming the industry. Autonomous trains augmented reality for maintenance and repairs, and the integration of AI for efficient train operations are some of the advancements we will look into.

As we move forward, the face of railway transportation continues to evolve, offering us glimpses of a future where borders become even less significant. As a result, the world becomes a closer, more connected place.

5

Railways - Connecting Landscapes and Cultures

Trains and Tourism: Scenic Rail Routes

The symbiosis between trains and tourism is beautifully showcased by scenic rail routes across the globe. Each journey is a testament to human achievement, perfectly blending into nature's spectacle. For instance, the Glacier Express in Switzerland travels through alpine landscapes, showcasing pristine mountains, sprawling meadows, and enchanting valleys. The nine-hour journey through the Swiss Alps doesn't just offer spectacular views; it weaves a narrative that captures the spirit of Switzerland, promoting cultural understanding and influencing tourism on a substantial scale.

In Asia, the Trans-Siberian Railway in Russia, the world's longest railway line, offers a unique insight into the Russian heartland, Siberian wilderness, and Mongolian steppe, creating an immersive cultural experience that far outweighs any language barrier. The journey lasts a week, and the train becomes a temporary home. This unique selling proposition draws tourists worldwide and significantly boosts the local economy.

The Blue Train of South Africa offers luxury and adventure on a different continent. Traversing South Africa's diverse landscapes, from the savannahs of Pretoria to the modern topography of Cape Town, the Blue Train offers a unique vantage point into the African wilderness while promising the comfort of a five-star hotel.

These scenic rail routes, and many more, significantly contribute to their respective countries' tourism industries. They offer tourists a unique, in-depth view of the countries' heartlands that few other modes of transportation can provide. They also encourage sustainable tourism practices by reducing carbon footprints, a significant draw for environmentally conscious travelers in our era of climate change awareness. As such, these trains are not just modes of transportation, but cultural ambassadors, environmental stewards, and significant economic boosters.

Trains and Social Impact

Trains have profoundly impacted society and culture, serving as catalysts for change and instruments of connection. When the first locomotives began to traverse countries and continents, they didn't just ferry goods and passengers—they connected communities, cities, and entire nations. Trains effectively shrank the world, making travel and communication faster and easier, a reality we often take for granted today.

In the United States, constructing the transcontinental railway in the 19th century was a landmark event. It connected the industrialized East with the rural West, enabling goods, services, and people to move freely across vast distances. This had immense societal impacts—it encouraged westward expansion, spurred economic growth, and even influenced the course of the American Civil War.

Trains also had a significant role in the industrialization process in Europe. By providing a reliable, efficient means of transporting goods and people, they transformed the industrial landscape, catalyzing the shift from an agricultural to an industrial society. They also facilitated urbanization, with towns growing around train stations, ultimately morphing into bustling cities.

In India, the extensive rail network established during the British Raj period profoundly shaped the country's social and economic fabric. It allowed for the movement of goods and people across vast distances, bridging cultural and geographical divides and fostering a sense of national unity. To this day, Indian Railways remains an essential part of the country's social structure, playing a vital role in daily life.

Moreover, trains have significantly impacted the arts and popular culture. From mystery novels set on glamorous European express trains, such as Agatha Christie's "Murder on the Orient Express," to films showcasing India's vibrant rail culture, like "The Darjeeling Limited," trains have provided a unique backdrop to numerous stories, influencing our collective imagination.

In essence, the impact of trains on our world is vast and multifaceted. They have shaped our physical landscapes and profoundly impacted our social, economic, and cultural landscapes. They continue to serve as indispensable links, connecting us in more ways than one.

Trains in Popular Culture

Trains hold a special place in popular culture, with their presence often used to symbolize journey, change, or even destiny. Their influence spans films, literature, music, and even painting, imprinting the collective human imagination with their raw power and romantic charm.

In cinema, trains have been central to many memorable scenes. Alfred Hitchcock's 'North by Northwest utilizes trains as a key plot device, as does the iconic James Bond film 'From Russia with Love.' More recently, the Korean movie 'Snowpiercer' imagines a post-apocalyptic world on a train. In India, Bollywood films often depict dramatic scenes at railway stations or aboard the trains themselves, with the Indian Railways being almost synonymous with the country's cinematic journey.

Literature is also rich with train symbolism. Agatha Christie's 'Murder on the Orient Express' and J.K. Rowling's 'Harry Potter' series, with its magical Hogwarts Express, are just some examples. In both cases, the train plays a vital role in the narrative, adding a sense of motion, transition, and adventure to the plot.

Music, too, has been touched by the allure of trains. Johnny Cash's 'Folsom Prison Blues,' with its famous opening line,

"I hear the train a-coming," or Gladys Knight & the Pips' 'Midnight Train to Georgia,' are tracks where trains are integral to the lyrics' imagery. They often symbolize escape, movement, or a return to roots.

In painting, trains have been captured in various ways, such as the romantic depictions of steam trains by artists during the Industrial Revolution or the more modern representations in graffiti art on subway trains.

As symbolic entities, trains often represent power, industry, and human progress. Still, they also evoke a sense of nostalgia, a longing for a bygone era. Trains' unique dichotomy makes them a versatile motif in popular culture that continues to inspire and captivate audiences worldwide.

6

Conclusion

The Enduring Romance of Railways

In the collective human consciousness, trains evoke nostalgia and romance, a sense of journey, and the thrill of exploration. From the earliest steam engines puffing through verdant countryside to the modern high-speed rail systems cutting across diverse landscapes, trains have captivated our imaginations and hearts. They embody progress and adventure, connecting places, people, cultures, and stories.

Despite advancements in other forms of transportation, the enduring allure of trains remains. There's something inherently magical about a train ride, whether it's the rhythm of wheels clattering on the tracks, the sweeping views flashing by the window, or the quaint charm of station stops. Trains offer us a way to slow down, to savor the journey as much as the destination.

In this rapidly changing world, trains remind us of the importance of connections - not just physical but also social and emotional. They have become symbols of shared journeys and experiences, a metaphor for life with its myriad destinations and fellow travelers.

As we roll beyond the horizon, it's clear that trains will continue to hold a special place in our world. They will evolve and adapt, embracing new technologies and possibilities, yet their fundamental essence will remain. Trains are not just modes of transport; they are part of our cultural heritage, collective memory, and shared dreams of exploration and discovery. They are, indeed, a romance that endures.

The Future of Trains and Railways

As we look toward the future, it becomes evident that trains and rail travel will continue to play a critical role in the world's transportation ecosystem. New technologies, changing societal norms, and an increasing focus on environmental sustainability are all set to influence the future trajectory of rail transportation.

Advancements in technology hold immense potential for trans-forming train travel. Magnetic levitation, or Maglev trains, which use magnets to hover above the tracks and move at incredibly high speeds, are already a reality in some parts of the world. Concepts like Elon Musk's Hyperloop propose a paradigm shift in rail transportation, with passenger pods traveling near-supersonic speeds in low-pressure tubes. Automation and artificial intelligence are set to make train operations more efficient and safer with autonomous trains and intelligent track systems.

The future of trains is not just about speed and technology; it's also about sustainability. As concerns about climate change and environmental degradation intensify, trains offer an energy-efficient and relatively low-carbon alternative to air and road travel. Innovations in train design and operation, such as lighter materials, aerodynamic techniques, regenerative braking, and renewable energy sources, could further reduce the environmental impact of trains.

Changes in societal norms and lifestyles will also influence the future of trains. As people become more environmentally conscious and look for ways to reduce their carbon footprint, they may increasingly turn to trains for short-distance commuting and long-distance travel. Trains also offer the possibility of more spacious and comfortable travel compared to planes and cars, with amenities like dining cars, sleeping compartments, and Wi-Fi making train travel more appealing.

While we cannot predict the future, one thing is clear: trains and railways are here to stay. They will continue to connect places and people, shaping landscapes and cultures. They will continue inspiring, fascinating, and transporting us to new horizons. As we stand at the platform, waiting for the future to arrive, we can be sure it will be a fascinating journey.

Appendix

Glossary of Train Terminology

This glossary provides a basic understanding of standard railway terms. As the world of trains is vast and diverse, there are countless more terms and concepts to explore. The learning journey is like a train journey, full of excitement and discovery at every turn.

- **Bogie**: A framework carrying wheels attached to a carriage or locomotive.
- **Caboose**: A car at the end of a freight train used by the crew.
- **Diesel-Electric Locomotive**: A locomotive that uses a diesel engine to generate electricity that drives electric motors which turn the wheels.
- **Gauge**: The distance between the inner sides of the rails on a track.
- **Light Rail**: Urban rail transit employs rolling stock akin to a tram; however, it operates with higher passenger capacity and is typically on a dedicated exclusive track.
- **Locomotive**: The vehicle that provides the motive power for a train.
- **Maglev**: Short for magnetic levitation. A groundbreaking train system utilizing dual sets of magnets. One set propels

the train upwards by repelling it from the track. In contrast, the other set drives the elevated train forward seamlessly.

- **Monorail**: A railway system where the train runs on a single rail, often elevated, and sometimes monorails run on straddle-beam tracks.
- **Rolling Stock**: All vehicles that move on a railway.
- **Sleeper**: A railroad car with beds for sleeping passengers.
- **Steam Engine**: An engine that uses steam's expansion or rapid condensation to generate power.
- **Track Ballast**: The material that holds the railway track in place and helps drainage.
- **Tram**: A rail vehicle on tramway tracks along public urban streets; some include segments of segregated right-of-way.
- **Turntable**: A device for turning railway stock, usually locomotives, so they can be moved back the way they came.
- **Yard**: A complex series of railway tracks for storing, sorting, or loading/unloading railroad cars or locomotives.

Further Exploration

Here is a selection of recommended materials for those who wish to learn more about the fascinating world of trains:

Books

The Great Railroad Revolution by Christian Wolmar: This book is a comprehensive history of trains in America and how they transformed the country economically, socially, and culturally.

Riding the Iron Rooster by Paul Theroux: Theroux, a renowned travel writer, recounts his journey by train across the vast expanse of China.

The Last Train to Zona Verd* by Paul Theroux: In this book, Theroux explores Africa through an epic journey by rail.

The Old Patagonian Express* by Paul Theroux: The author describes his train journey from Boston to Patagonia, passing through several South American countries.

Articles

The Future of Rail: Opportunities for Energy and the Environment* (IEA, 2019): An article that discusses the role of trains in a sustainable future.

High-speed rail and economic development: The case of China* (World Bank, 2019): This report explores the economic impact of high-speed rail in China.

Documentaries

The Race Underground* (PBS, 2017): This documentary tells the story of the technological and social innovations that led to the creation of America's first subway system.

The Indian Pacific: Australia's Longest Train Journey* (Slow TV, 2018): A unique television experience capturing a four-day journey across Australia.

Extreme Railways (Channel 5, 2012-2016): This documentary series showcases some of the world's most incredible and dangerous railways.

These resources should provide a rich understanding of the past, present, and future of trains and railway systems around the globe.

Call to Action

Your journey through the captivating world of trains doesn't have to end with the last page of this book. One of the most rewarding aspects of writing is hearing from you, the readers. Your thoughts, ideas, and feedback help us shape future work and inspire us to delve deeper into the topics you find most intriguing.

If you've enjoyed this journey beyond the horizon and into the fascinating world of trains, please take a few minutes and share your thoughts on Amazon. Reviews help other potential readers decide whether the book might be right for them and provide valuable insights that can help improve future editions.

Your feedback, whether a few words or a detailed review, is greatly appreciated. Let's continue to explore and learn together, one track at a time.

Thank you for being so supportive, and Happy Reading!

Resources

Ambrose, S. E. (2000). Nothing Like It in the World: The Men Who Built the Transcontinental Railroad 1863-1869. Simon & Schuster.

Burton, A. (1992). The Railway Empire. Palgrave Macmillan.

Cervero, R. (1998). The Transit Metropolis: A Global Inquiry. Island Press.

Christiansen, R. (1995). The Great Western at Work 1921-1939. Patrick Stephens Ltd.

Encyclopedia Britannica. (2023). Train. Retrieved July 21, 2023, from https://www.britannica.com/technology/train.

European Railway Agency. (2023). Rail safety. Retrieved July 21, 2023, from https://www.era.europa.eu/.

Flanders, S. (2009). The Railway Journey: The Industrialization of Time and Space. University of California Press.

Freeman, M. (2012). Railways and the Victorian Imagination. Yale University Press.

History of Trains Website. (2023). History of Trains. Retrieved July 21, 2023, from http://www.trainhistory.net/.

Hood, C. P. (2006). Shinkansen: From Bullet Train to Symbol of Modern Japan. Routledge.

How Trains Work. (2023). How Trains Work. Retrieved July 21, 2023, from https://www.howtrainswork.com/.

International Union of Railways. (2023). UIC Passenger. Retrieved July 21, 2023, from https://uic.org/.

Kerr, I. (2007). Railways in Modern India. Oxford University Press.

Simmons, J. (2003). The Victorian Railway. Thames & Hudson Ltd.

Smil, V. (2010). Prime Movers of Globalization: The History and Impact of Diesel Engines and Gas Turbines. The MIT Press.

Solomon, B. (2011). Railroad Signaling. Voyageur Press.

Stover, J. F. (1997). American Railroads. The University of Chicago Press.

The National Railway Museum. (2023). The National Railway Museum. Retrieved July 21, 2023, from https://www.railwaymuseum.org.uk/.

Wolmar, C. (2008). Fire and Steam: A New History of the

Railways in Britain. Atlantic Books.

World Bank. (2023). Railways. Retrieved July 21, 2023, from https://www.worldbank.org/en/topic/transport/brief/rail.

www.ingramcontent.com/pod-product-compliance
Lightning Source LLC
Chambersburg PA
CBHW061328120626
46546CB00007B/2724